UNWAVERING LOVE

Truth That Holds

Ralph McCall

Think Deep! Series

destinēe

COPYRIGHT

Unwavering Love: Truth That Holds
By Ralph McCall

© Copyright 2025 by Ralph McCall

All rights reserved. No part of this publication may be reproduced, distributed, or transmitted in any form or by any means, including photocopying, recording, or other electronic or mechanical methods, without the prior written permission of the publisher, except in the case of brief quotations embodied in critical reviews and specific other noncommercial uses permitted by copyright law.

English Standard Version (ESV) © Crossway Bibles. Used by permission. All rights reserved.

New International Version (NIV) © Biblica, Inc. Used by permission. All rights reserved worldwide.

New King James Version (NKJV)

Published by Destinee Media, www.destineemedia.com
Written by Ralph McCall

ISBN: 978-1-938367-95-3

CONTENTS

Copyright ii
Contents iii
Think Deep! Series iv
INTRODUCTION — A HOPE WORTH THINKING DEEPLY
ABOUT 1
CHAPTER 1 — WHEN EVERYTHING FEELS UNSTABLE 3
CHAPTER 2 — IF TRUTH IS REAL, WHAT KIND OF GOD
MUST THERE BE? 12
CHAPTER 3 — THE WOUND WE CANNOT HEAL 21
CHAPTER 4 — JESUS: THE RESCUE WE COULD NEVER
CREATE 29
CHAPTER 5 — FAITH & GRACE: RECEIVING WHAT CHRIST
HAS DONE 37
CHAPTER 6: THE INVITATION — TURNING FROM
SHADOWS TO LIGHT 43
CONCLUSION — THE DOOR IS OPEN 49
Further Reading 57
Think Deep! Series 58

THINK DEEP! SERIES

Unwavering Love: Truth That Holds is part of the **Think Deep! Series**, created for those who want more than surface answers.

Each book in the series explores the big questions about culture, identity, and faith—designed for a digital generation immersed in an endless array of perspectives and ever-shifting narratives.

To develop true and just discernment.

INTRODUCTION — A HOPE WORTH THINKING DEEPLY ABOUT

This book is about hope.
About unwavering love.
About truth that holds when everything else feels unsteady.

You're holding a journey that speaks to the deepest questions people carry but rarely voice—the desire for stability, for meaning, for something real enough to live by and strong enough to rest in.

If you've been longing for clarity in a world crowded with noise, you're in the right place.

But hope becomes stronger when we first understand why we need it.
And that's where our journey begins.

Chapter 1 invites you to slow down and reflect on the tension beneath modern life—the pressure, the uncertainty, the quiet ache we all sense but seldom name. It isn't meant to discourage you; it's meant to prepare you.

Because when we think deeply and honestly about the world as it is, we become able to see something far greater than the world as it seems.

After we examine the condition of our culture, we turn toward something profoundly positive

a truth strong enough to steady your identity,

a foundation that does not shift with feelings or trends,

a hope durable enough to carry the weight of a real human life.

The chapters that follow move from clarity to comfort, from diagnosis to direction, from the instability of our moment to the kind of certainty every generation longs for. You will not be asked to create meaning out of thin air, or to rely on your emotions to guide your future. Instead, you'll be invited to discover something far more trustworthy.

As you read, expect a journey that grows brighter as it goes.

- Expect to encounter ideas that steady the heart.

- Expect a vision of life that is larger, stronger, and more life-giving than the one our culture offers.

- Expect to find a truth you can build on.

The Book of Proverbs says that surely there is a future and a hope. That's what we are after.

This book begins by letting you see the cracks—
but it ends by showing you the Cornerstone.

Let's begin.

CHAPTER 1 — WHEN EVERYTHING FEELS UNSTABLE

There are moments — usually the quiet ones — when life feels shaky in a way you can't quite name.

Not a crisis.

Not a disaster.

Just a subtle, constant wobble underneath everything.

> You feel it when the noise fades.

> You feel it when the distractions stop working.

> You feel it when you're finally honest with yourself.

It's the sense that the world around you keeps shifting... and the world inside you shifts with it. Deep down, you wonder: What am I supposed to hold onto when everything keeps moving?

This chapter is about that trembling place — and what it reveals.

---

1. The Life We Build Eventually Starts Cracking

Most people don't wake up one morning and say, "I need truth."

They simply feel the pressure of a life that's losing shape.

You've probably felt it too:

- You try to be authentic, but your identity keeps changing.
- You try to be confident, but the confidence never stays.

- You try to feel whole, but the wholeness dissolves by morning.

So you do what everyone does in a culture like ours:

You try to stabilize yourself with experiences, emotions, people, routines, and "your truth."

You optimize your productivity. You curate your social media. You chase the next promotion, the next vacation, the next achievement. You build a comfortable life with good friends, decent work, and enough entertainment to fill the empty spaces.

For a while, it works.

Until it doesn't.

And eventually, quiet questions rise:

> If my truth keeps shifting, how can it hold the weight of my life?

> If the ground inside me is unstable, what can I stand on?

---

2. The Emotional Weight of "My Truth"

We were told that freedom comes from looking inward — finding our own meaning, defining our own reality, choosing our own identity.

It sounds empowering.

But living it out can be exhausting.

Because if you are the source of truth, then you are also the support beam for your entire world.

And here's the part no one talks about:

A human heart is too fragile to carry that much responsibility.

- We weren't built to invent reality from scratch.
- We weren't designed to be our own foundation.
- We weren't meant to create a world and then try to hold it up alone.

And you know this. You feel it.

The pressure to self-create eventually becomes the pressure to self-sustain — and no one can do that forever.

And if you've tried to sustain yourself through **spiritual practices**—manifestation, crystals, energy work, aligning with the universe—you know an even deeper exhaustion. Because now you're not just creating your own meaning; you're performing your own transcendence. You're checking your horoscope, pulling tarot cards, raising your vibration, clearing your chakras—always working, always adjusting, always wondering why the universe isn't responding the way you hoped.

The promise was cosmic connection. The reality is cosmic loneliness. Because the universe—whatever it is—cannot know you. Cannot speak to you. Cannot love you back.

So the question becomes:

What happens when "my truth" collapses under the weight of real life?

---

3. But What If You Don't Feel This Yet?

Maybe you're reading this and thinking:

"I don't feel that instability. My life is actually pretty good."

Or maybe you're thinking:

"This sounds like religious fear-mongering designed to make me feel broken so I'll need your God."

Fair enough.

If your life feels stable, if secular meaning is working for you, if relationships and career and comfort feel like enough—then hold onto that. Don't manufacture problems you don't have.

But, I bet things are not that together. There is always the "who am I" question.

And,

> What is my identity?
>
> What is love?
>
> Why do I feel hurt?
>
> Why did I feel injustice?
>
> Is there a God, and is he personal? What is he like?

Maybe you're reading because someone you love asked you to. Maybe you're intellectually curious about what Christians actually believe. Maybe you're here to debunk it. Maybe you picked it up by accident and haven't put it down yet.

Whatever your reason, you don't need to justify it. You're welcome here.

And if you're resistant because religion has hurt you—or because you've watched Christians be hypocrites—then you're right to be cautious. Christianity has often been used as a weapon. Jesus knows that better than anyone. (They crucified Him for it.)

But that doesn't make Jesus wrong. It makes religion dangerous when mishandled.

The invitation here isn't to join a religious system. It's to consider whether the story of Jesus might be true—independent of whether Christians have represented Him well.

You don't have to manufacture an ache to keep reading. Just curiosity is enough.

---

4. The Logical End of a Self-Made Worldview

If you follow postmodern spirituality to its end, it leads somewhere unexpected:

> If everyone has their own truth… then no one's truth means anything.
>
> If meaning is something we create… then meaning can disappear the moment we stop believing in it.
>
> If morality is subjective… then betrayal, cruelty, and injustice lose all grounding — even when they devastate us.

This is where relativism collapses on itself.

Because eventually, you feel something that doesn't fit the theory: You know some things are actually wrong.

---

5. The Personal Cracks No One Can Escape

Everyone has a moment — sometimes small, sometimes shattering — when life exposes the fault lines.

> A breakup.

A betrayal.

A sleepless night.

A sudden loneliness.

A promotion that feels empty.

A vacation that doesn't refresh.

A Netflix queue that never satisfies.

A weekend that passes without meaning.

A moment when the crystals don't work.

A night when manifestation feels like self-deception.

A realization that the universe never actually speaks back.

A guilt that maybe you're the reason your energy is blocked.

A joy that fades faster than it should.

And in that moment, you realize: **"Self-constructed meaning can't comfort me. My truth can't carry me. The universe doesn't answer back."**

You don't need philosophy to feel that.

Your own story tells you. Because when your internal world shakes, you want something that doesn't shake.

When your emotions collapse, you want something steadier than emotions.

When your truth falls apart, you want the truth — something outside you, above you, greater than you.

And that desire isn't weakness.

It's honesty.

It's the most human thing about you.

---

6. What Your Longing Is Trying to Tell You (Even If You Haven't Named It Yet)

You may not realize it, but your ache is not random.

It's a message.

A signal.

A whisper from somewhere (from someone) beyond you.

> Every time you long for meaning…
>
> every time you refuse to accept that love is just chemicals…
>
> every time justice feels more than a preference…
>
> every time beauty feels like a clue…

Your soul is saying:

"There must be more than this."

And if there must be more than this, then maybe "more" isn't a what. Maybe it's a who.

Relativism can't answer that longing.

New Age spirituality can't ground it.

Self-help can't fix it.

Your truth can't sustain it.

But you're not wrong for feeling it.

You're awake.

---

7. Where This Chapter Has Been Leading

If everything inside you is unstable —

and everything around you is unstable —

then looking inward forever will only lead to more instability.

You need something outside you.

> Something greater than you.

> Something real, objective, unchanging, personal, and true.

> Something strong enough to build your life on.

This chapter has been about identifying the cracks.

The next chapters are about discovering the foundation.

Because if truth exists…

and if it is bigger than you… then it must come from somewhere. From someone.

Truth that is real, objective, and unchanging can't emerge from shifting human opinions. It can't be voted on. It can't evolve with culture. It can't be invented.

If truth is real, it must have a source.

And that source must be personal—because impersonal forces don't create meaning, morality, beauty, or love. Only persons do.

So the question becomes:

What kind of God must there be—if truth exists and if He is its source?

And the most importantly: If God exists, how can we know him?

And what would it mean if He is reaching toward you?

Whether you feel the instability now, whether you're coasting comfortably, or whether you're skeptical of this entire conversation—the next chapter is for you. Because the question isn't whether YOU need truth. The question is whether truth exists. And if it does, what kind of God must be behind it.

That's where we go next.

CHAPTER 2 — IF TRUTH IS REAL, WHAT KIND OF GOD MUST THERE BE?

The Quiet Question Behind Every Honest Search

When the noise finally dies down…
when the opinions fade…
when "my truth" stops holding you up…
a quiet question slips in:

**If truth is real…
where does it come from?**

**In the Bible…
God reveals Himself not only as truth,
but as *the* truth.**

What does that mean?

Most people don't start with God.
They start with a feeling:

A moment of honesty after a breakup.
A moment of clarity at 3 A.M.
A moment when the self you curated online feels paper-thin.
A moment when the life you've built feels like it can't hold your weight anymore.

And suddenly you're asking things you don't usually ask:

Why do I long for love that doesn't leave?

Why do I expect justice in a world that says morality is relative?

Why does guilt still feel real even when culture tells me I shouldn't feel it?

Questions like these don't appear out of nowhere.
They rise from deep inside you.
And they are clues — quiet ones — pointing to Someone beyond you.

Because if truth exists…
and meaning exists…
and morality exists…
and beauty moves you…
and love changes you…

Then none of those things can be accidents.
They are not inventions.
They are revelations.

And revelations point somewhere.

---

1. Why "the Universe" Isn't Enough

If you scroll through Instagram or TikTok long enough, you'll see it:

"Trust the universe."
"Manifest your future."
"Send energy into the cosmos."
"Listen to the vibe."

And it feels safe, doesn't it?
Because a cosmic force never confronts you.
Never challenges you.
Never speaks to you.
Never sees the parts of you you try to hide.

But there's a problem:

> **A force can't love you.**

> **A force can't forgive you.**

A force can't comfort you.

A force can't answer you in the dark.

A force can't tell you who you are.

The universe isn't a *who*.
It's a *what*.

A cosmic force is emotionally convenient…
but spiritually useless.

A warm energy can't guide you.
A vibe can't rescue you.
A feeling can't define right and wrong.

As C.S. Lewis once noted,
impersonal gods are comfortable because they demand nothing.

But comfort without reality is just illusion.

If the ache inside you is real,
if your longing is real,
then the answer must also be real —

You need someone personal.

---

2. God Is Personal — Not a Force, Not a Feeling

The Bible never describes God as an idea or a mood.
God speaks.
God hears.
God loves.
God wills.
God calls.
God reveals Himself.

He is "I AM" (Exodus 3:14) —
the self-existing, personal Being behind everything.

As theologian John Frame said:

"God is not a principle. God is the Lord."

This means:

Your life is not an accident.

Your worth is not self-manufactured.

Your value is not fragile.

Your identity is not something you assemble from scratch.

You were designed.

You were meant for relationship.
Not with the universe.
But with a Person.

This is why Christianity is so different from modern spirituality:

You are not climbing toward God.
God is coming toward you.

---

3. God Is Holy — The One We Cannot Tame

If God is personal, then who He is actually matters.
And the first word Scripture uses to describe Him is this:

Holy.

"Holy, holy, holy is the Lord of hosts." — Isaiah 6:3

Holiness means God is not like us.
Not corruptible.
Not confused.
Not fragile.
Not manipulated by emotion or ego.

He is perfect in purity.
Radiant in goodness.
Beautiful in righteousness.

It means God is unique and separate from us and the world.

This is the part of God that modern spirituality tries to avoid —
because
Holiness confronts.
Holiness exposes.
Holiness reveals who we really are.

But holiness is not cruelty.
It is beauty.

Holiness is why justice exists.
Holiness is why love is reliable.
Holiness is why evil will not win.
Holiness is why heaven is pure joy.

As R.C. Sproul wrote:

"The holiness of God is traumatic to unholy people."

And yet —
this Holy God draws near.

Holiness isn't a barrier.
It's the doorway through which real love enters the world.

---

4. God Is Loving — Not Soft, But Sacrificial

People often picture God as angry, distant, or disappointed. But Scripture paints something far more surprising:

"God is love." — 1 John 4:8

Love is not God's hobby.
It is His nature.

But His love is not the sentimental love of modern culture.

It is not soft.

It is not enabling.

It does not shrug at sin.

It does not whisper, "Do whatever makes you happy."

True love confronts what destroys.
True love sacrifices.
True love heals.

"God shows His love for us in that while we were still sinners, Christ died for us." — Romans 5:8

This is holy love —
love that sees your brokenness and moves toward you anyway.

And true love is what we all desire, **Unwavering Love**.

The universe cannot love like that.
A feeling cannot love like that.
Only a Person can.

5. God Reveals Himself — We Do Not Guess Our Way to Him

If God is personal, holy, and loving, then we cannot invent Him. He must reveal Himself.

And He has.

- **In creation** — His power (Psalm 19:1)
- **In Scripture** — His character (2 Timothy 3:16)
- **In Jesus Christ** — His heart (John 1:18)

Theologian Herman Bavinck wrote:

"God is the One who interprets Himself."

We don't guess who God is.
We don't build Him from our preferences.
We don't assemble Him from vibes.
We don't climb toward Him through spiritual effort.

> **He speaks.**
>
> **He initiates.**
>
> **He discloses.**
>
> **He comes near.**

All you are doing is listening.

---

6. God's Nearness — A Personal God Who Draws Close

Perhaps the most shocking claim of Christianity is this:

**The holy God who created galaxies
draws near to people like us.**

"The Lord is near to all who call on Him." — *Psalm 145:18*

Not the impressive.
Not the spiritual elite.
Not the perfect.

The broken.
The questioning.
The restless.
The ones who can no longer pretend they're okay.

The God who is holy is also the God who is love.

The God who is infinite is also the God who is near.

The God who is personal is also the God who is pursuing you.

You don't need to manifest His presence.
You don't need to perform for His attention.
You don't need to convince Him to care.

He already moved toward you.
He is already speaking.
He is already inviting.

The Door That This Opens

Once you see the cracks in "my truth"
and once you realize the universe cannot love you
and once you sense the pull of a God who is personal, holy, loving, and near…

A new question rises:

If such a God exists… why do I feel so far from Him?

That question leads directly into the next chapter:

What went wrong — and what God has already done to make it right.

CHAPTER 3 — THE WOUND WE CANNOT HEAL

Why We Feel Far From a God Who Is Near

If Chapter 2 showed us a God who is holy, loving, and personal…
then a new question naturally rises:

**If God is like that,
why do we feel so far from Him?**

Why does life feel fractured?
Why do our hearts feel conflicted?
Why does guilt cling to us even when we deny morality?
Why do we sabotage ourselves even when we genuinely want to do better?

Every honest person eventually reaches this point.
The ache inside you is not random.
It is not just trauma or culture or circumstances.

It is something deeper —
something the Bible names with unsettling clarity.

This chapter isn't here to crush you.
It's here to tell the truth you've already felt in your own soul.
Because until you understand the problem,
you will never understand the rescue.

1. Something Is Wrong With Us — And We Know It

You don't need a Bible to know this.
Every human feels the fracture.

> The guilt you can't shake

The secrets you replay

The habits you can't break

The emptiness success can't fill

The self-sabotage you can't explain

It's the experience Paul describes:

***"For I do not do the good I want,
but the evil I do not want is what I keep on doing."***
— *Romans 7:19*

It's like trying to steer a car with a bent frame.
No matter how tightly you grip the wheel,
your life drifts toward the ditch.

Something in us is bent —
not slightly, but deeply.

We aren't just wounded.
We are wired wrong.

---

2. The Bible's Diagnosis: A Sin Nature

Culture says:
"I make mistakes."
The Bible says:
"I am sinful."

Culture says:
"I'm trying my best."
The Bible says:
"The heart is deceitful above all things."
— *Jeremiah 17:9*

Culture says:
"People are basically good."
The Bible says:
"None is righteous, no, not one."
— *Romans 3:10*

This is not about shame.
It's about honesty.

Theologian **John Murray** explains it perfectly:

"Sin is not merely an act; it is a condition out of which acts arise."

We don't become sinners by sinning.
We sin because we are sinners.

King David admitted this with painful clarity:

"Surely I was sinful at birth…
sinful from the time my mother conceived me."
— *Psalm 51:5*

This isn't poetry.
It's diagnosis.

---

3. A Broken Backpack — Not Just Damaged, Defective

Imagine you buy a backpack.
But it has a factory flaw.
Even empty, the seams tear.
Even gently used, the straps snap.

That's humanity.

We aren't just damaged by life.
We are *defective at the core* —
unable to carry the weight we were designed for.

We buckle under guilt.
We tear under shame.
We collapse under expectations.
We come apart under desire, fear, and loneliness.

Not because life is too heavy…
but because our nature is too broken.

You don't need a motivational speech.
You need a rebuild.

Not new habits.
A new heart.

---

4. Sin Is Not Just Breaking Rules — It's Breaking Relationship

Most people think sin is doing bad things.
The Bible goes deeper.

Sin is **relational rebellion**:

> Distrusting God's goodness

> Ignoring His voice

> Preferring other loves

> Choosing autonomy over intimacy

> Saying (quietly or loudly),
> *"I'll run my life my way."*

Every sin begins with the same lie:

"I know better than God."

It's to say, "I am God," which was the tragic error in the Garden of Eden.

We don't trust Him.
So we trust ourselves —
the very selves that hurt us most.

Sin makes us not just guilty.
It makes us spiritually dead.

---

5. Spiritual Death — Our Deepest Problem

Paul says it plainly:

"You were dead in your trespasses and sins."
— *Ephesians 2:1*

Not confused.
Not mildly flawed.
Not spiritually sleepy.
Dead.

A dead person can't revive himself.
A spiritually dead person cannot crawl toward God,
cannot choose God by willpower,
cannot heal their own nature,
cannot rescue themselves.

This is the Reformed doctrine of **total depravity** —
not that we are as bad as possible,
but that every part of us is infected.

Theologian **Charles Hodge** wrote:

"Sin is not merely an act; it is a state of the soul."

A dead soul needs resurrection —
not motivation.

---

6. "But I'm a Good Person" — The Most Comforting Illusion

Most people say they are "basically good."

But goodness is not measured against other people.
Goodness is measured against God.

"For all have sinned and fall short of the glory of God."
— Romans 3:23

Imagine this:

After you die, you stand before God, who is the judge,
And He asks, "Why should I have anything to do with you? —
And "Why should I let you into my heaven?"

And you answer,
"I've been a good person."

And God answers,

"For whoever keeps the whole law and yet stumbles at just one point is guilty of breaking all of it." James 2:10

That shows how holy God is. That shows how high the bar is set.

Even our best moments are mixed with pride, insecurity, fear, or self-interest.

We are cracked mirrors.
We reflect goodness —
but always distorted.

We need a new mirror.
A new nature.

---

7. Sin Creates Separation — Not Just Shame

Sin isn't only a feeling of guilt.
It is a relational rupture.

"Your iniquities have separated you from your God."
— Isaiah 59:2

God is holy.
We are not.
And holiness and sin cannot share the same space.

This is why spirituality cannot fix us.
This is why self-help cannot fix us.
This is why religion cannot fix us.

We are separated from God, and we can't bridge the gap.

That's the problem with religion, in all its forms. They all try to find a back door to fulfillment, to heaven, whether Eastern, New Age, Mysticism, or any other form. This idea of doing spiritual things, of working your way to God, even shows up in Christianity.

The reality is that no religious or human acts can get us into a relationship with a perfect, holy God.

No one climbs out of spiritual death.

If rescue exists,
it must come from outside.

8. Why This Hard News Is Actually Good News

At first, this chapter feels heavy.
Dark.
Uncomfortable.

But this is where hope begins.

Because if the problem is deeper than your mistakes,
then the solution must be deeper than your effort.

You cannot heal yourself —
but **Someone** can.

As Tim Keller wrote:

*"We are more sinful and flawed than we ever dared believe,
yet more loved and accepted in Christ than we ever dared hope."*

You cannot fix this wound.
But you can be healed.

And that is where the story turns next:

**If we cannot climb our way to God,
what if God has already climbed down to us?**

CHAPTER 4 — JESUS: THE RESCUE WE COULD NEVER CREATE

If Chapter 3 showed the wound we cannot heal, this chapter shows the rescue we could never earn, build, or even imagine.

Because if sin is our deepest problem, then the question becomes unavoidable:

Who can rescue us from ourselves?

Not self-help.
Not religion.
Not therapy alone.
Not spiritual vibes or "good energy."
Not moral effort, self-improvement, or becoming "your best self."

We cannot climb out of spiritual death.
We cannot repair a broken nature.
We cannot erase guilt, heal shame, or resurrect our own souls.

If a rescue is possible, it must come from outside us.

And the shocking claim of Christianity is this:

Someone has come.
Someone stepped into our world.
Someone carried what we could never carry.
Someone took on our death so we could receive His life.

His name is Jesus.

1. The Real Jesus — Not the Trend, Not the Aesthetic

Ask ten people who Jesus is, and you will hear ten different answers:

- "A wise teacher."
- "A revolutionary."
- "A spiritual influencer."
- "A moral example."
- "A symbol of love."

But these versions of Jesus are too small.
They shrink Him into someone we can admire without obeying… quote without surrendering… reference without trusting.

The real Jesus refuses to fit into our categories.

The real Jesus is the **God-Man**—fully God, fully human.
The eternal Son who stepped into space and time, the One through whom all things were made (John 1:3), the One who sustains the universe by His word (Hebrews 1:3).

He did not come to inspire you.
He came to rescue you.

He is not an influencer.
He is not an energy.
He is not a symbol.
He is not a mascot for religion.

He is **God in the flesh**, moving toward sinners with a love stronger than death.

2. The Incarnation — God Came Down

Christianity makes a claim unlike any other worldview:

God came down.
Not symbolically.
Not metaphorically.
Not disguised.
Literally.

"The Word became flesh and dwelt among us." — John 1:14

The infinite stepped into limits.
The eternal entered time.
The holy walked among sinners.

Alexander Maclaren captured this beautifully:

"Christ's life is God spelling Himself out in language we can understand."

God did not send an angel, a prophet, or a messenger.

He came Himself.

Why?
Because our problem was too deep for anyone else.

If we were only misguided, God could have sent a teacher.
If we were only wounded, He could have sent a healer.
But we were **dead**.

So He sent a **Savior**.

3. Jesus Lived the Life We Failed to Live

We were created to love God with our whole heart, soul, mind, and strength.
We haven't done this for a single day.

But Jesus did.

He obeyed perfectly.
He loved flawlessly.
He honored the Father in every thought, action, and motive.

He lived the life you were meant to live so He could give you the righteousness you could never earn.

"For our sake He made Him to be sin who knew no sin, so that in Him we might become the righteousness of God."
— 2 Corinthians 5:21

This is the first half of the **Divine Exchange**:

His obedience becomes yours.

---

4. Jesus Died the Death We Deserved

Sin always leads to death (Romans 6:23).
Judgment is not a glitch in God's character—it is an expression of His holiness and justice.

We sinned.
We turned away.
We broke the relationship.
Someone must bear the penalty.

And here is the miracle of the gospel:

The Judge took the judgment.
The King bore the curse.
The Shepherd died for the sheep.

The cross is not a symbol.
It is not an accident.
It is the central event in human history—the moment God's justice and love collided.

"This is love: not that we loved God, but that He loved us and sent His Son as the atoning sacrifice for our sins."
— 1 John 4:10

Jesus drank the full cup of God's righteous wrath so you would never taste a drop of it.

This is the second half of the Divine Exchange:

Your sin became His. His righteousness becomes yours.

---

5. The Cross Was Not Jesus' Defeat — It Was His Victory

From the outside, the cross looked like failure.
From the inside, it was triumph.

At the cross:

- Satan's accusation was silenced.

- Sin's power was broken.

- God's justice was satisfied.

- The door of mercy was opened once and for all.

He "disarmed the rulers and authorities and put them to open shame, by triumphing over them in Him."
— Colossians 2:15

The cross was not Jesus losing.
It was Jesus winning back His people, His creation, and your life.

---

6. The Resurrection — Death Defeated Once and for All

The resurrection is not a metaphor.
It is not a symbol of "new beginnings."
It is history. It is fact.

"God raised Him from the dead." — *Acts 2:24*

The resurrection means:

- Jesus is who He claimed to be.

- His sacrifice was accepted.

- Death has been defeated.

- Hope is real.

Tim Keller put it starkly:

"If Jesus rose from the dead, you must accept all He said. If He didn't, why worry about anything He said?"

The resurrection is the cosmic receipt—proof that Jesus paid the price in full.

---

7. Why Jesus Is the Only Way — Not "A Way"

Many people today want a spirituality without commitments.
A path without a Person.
A God without holiness.
A savior without authority.

But truth is not unkind—truth is a gift.

And here is the truth:

**If the world's greatest problem is sin, and only one Person paid for sin,
then only one Person can save.**

Jesus said:

"I am the way, the truth, and the life. No one comes to the Father except through Me."
— John 14:6

He didn't say, "I am one option among many."
He said, "I am the way."

Not because God is narrow.
But because **Jesus is the only One who dealt with the real problem**:

- Only Jesus is God in the flesh.

- Only Jesus lived perfectly.

- Only Jesus bore sin.

- Only Jesus satisfied justice.

- Only Jesus conquered death.

- Only Jesus reconciles a holy God and sinful people.

Other spiritual leaders offer **advice**.
Jesus offers **salvation**.
Others point toward the way.
Jesus **is** the way.

---

8. What This Means for You

If Jesus is who He says He is, then He is not optional.

He is not a spiritual supplement.
He is not a religious flavor.
He is not an accessory to your self-improvement journey.

He is the Savior you cannot live without
and the King you were created to follow.

He sees your sin.

He knows your secrets.

He understands your shame.

He feels your pain.

And He offers Himself freely—
not when you fix yourself,
not when you become "good,"
not when you try harder,
but **now**, exactly as you are.

CHAPTER 5 — FAITH & GRACE: RECEIVING WHAT CHRIST HAS DONE

If Chapter 4 is the heart of the gospel, this chapter is the pulse. Jesus lived for you, died for you, and rose for you — but that still leaves one question every honest reader must ask: *How does His rescue become mine?*

How does something that happened in history reach into my personal story, failures, fears, and shame?

The Bible gives two answers that always walk together: **Grace and Faith.**
Grace is God moving toward you, and faith is you opening your life to Him.

Grace is the cause; faith is the response.

Grace saves; faith receives.

This is why Scripture insists that salvation is *"by grace... through faith... not your own doing"* (Ephesians 2:8). God does the saving. We do the trusting.

---

1. Grace — God Moving Toward You

Most people think of grace as God lowering the bar, "cutting us slack," or being lenient because He knows we struggle.

But the biblical picture of grace is far more profound. **Grace is God doing for sinners what they could never do for themselves.**

It is God stepping toward rebels,

God pursuing runaways,

God rescuing those who cannot climb their way back.

Grace is God refusing to abandon people who abandoned Him. It is His goodness overpowering our weakness. It is His initiative, not ours.

Paul says it plainly:
"For by grace you have been saved... it is the gift of God."
— Ephesians 2:8

This means you didn't wake up one day and decide to get your life together. Grace awakened you. Grace moved first. Grace always moves first.

---

2. But Grace Is Not Soft — Grace Is Costly

Some imagine grace is God shrugging at sin. A kind of heavenly tolerance: "It's fine — nobody's perfect." But grace never trivializes sin.

Instead, grace takes sin so seriously that God gave His Son to bear it. That's what makes grace breathtaking. It doesn't ignore sin; it answers it.

John Stott put it well:
"Grace is love that cares enough to confront and then to forgive."

The cross shows both parts. Grace confronts sin — because Jesus had to die for it. And grace forgives sin — because Jesus willingly died for you.

Grace is free to you, but infinitely expensive to Christ.

This is why grace is not sentimental. It is sacrificial. It bleeds.

---

3. Faith — The Hand That Receives Grace

If grace is God extending His hand, faith is you opening yours.

Faith is not a heroic act. It's not spiritual talent or emotional certainty. It's not "trying harder to believe." Biblical faith is the simple, honest act of trusting Christ instead of trusting yourself.

Faith says:
"I cannot fix this.
I cannot save myself.
Jesus, I trust You to do what I cannot do."

Theologian Michael Horton described it beautifully:
"Faith is the empty hand of the sinner reaching out for the fullness of Christ."

That's why faith doesn't earn anything. Faith receives. Faith is not the price you pay. It is the posture that says, "I have nothing. He has everything."

---

4. Faith Is Not Blind — It Looks Directly at Jesus

People often talk about "having faith" as if faith is a vague positivity, a psychological trick, or a motivational slogan. But biblical faith always has an object: **Jesus Christ.**

Faith is only as reliable as the One it rests on.

That's why Christian faith doesn't look inward for strength; it looks outward to a Savior who already accomplished everything required.

Faith doesn't trust vibes.
Faith doesn't trust feelings.
Faith doesn't trust the universe.
Faith trusts the crucified and risen Lord.

And because Christ never changes, biblical faith never rests on shifting emotions — it rests on a finished work.

---

5. The Divine Exchange — The Heart of the Gospel

There is a reason Christians talk about the cross with awe. At the cross, something occurred that no religious system, spiritual technique, or human effort could ever produce.

You gave Jesus your sin, and Jesus gave you His righteousness.

This is the Divine Exchange.

Your sins and guilt → placed on Him.
Your death → absorbed by Him.
His life → given to you.
His righteousness → credited to you.

Martin Luther called this exchange "a wonderful transaction," writing:
"Our sins are no longer ours but Christ's, and Christ's righteousness is no longer His but ours."

This isn't metaphor. It is salvation.

God doesn't merely forgive your failures — He clothes you in Christ's perfection. Grace doesn't just wipe your slate clean. It writes Jesus' perfect record over your life.

And you receive that record through faith alone.

---

6. Faith Can Be Fragile — And Still Real

Sometimes your faith will feel small, shaky, clouded, or inconsistent. That's okay. Weak faith is still true faith when it rests on a strong Savior. Jesus said:

"A bruised reed He will not break, and a smoldering wick He will not snuff out."
— *Matthew 12:20*

This means your faith may flicker, but He will not abandon you.

What matters is not the strength of your grip on Christ — but the strength of Christ's grip on you.

---

7. Faith Is Not a Feeling — It Is Trust Anchored in Reality

Many young believers panic when the emotional rush fades. They think they've "lost their faith" because they don't feel spiritual. But faith was never built on feelings.

Feelings shift. Christ does not.

Biblical faith rests on facts:
A cross in history.
A tomb that is empty.
A Savior who lives.
A promise that stands.

Your emotional state may rise and fall, but God's grace does not move. Faith looks at Jesus, not at itself.

8. Grace Makes You New — Not Just Forgiven

Grace doesn't just wash your past. It remakes your future.
Grace doesn't only cleanse — it recreates.
Grace doesn't upgrade the old self — it gives you a new one.

Paul writes:
"If anyone is in Christ, he is a new creation."
— 2 Corinthians 5:17

This means God doesn't merely repair you. He rebirths you. You become someone you never could have made yourself.

Your identity is no longer shaped by your habits, failures, shame, or trauma. It is anchored in Christ Himself.

---

9. Grace Makes Salvation Certain

Some Christians imagine salvation is fragile — like God saved them reluctantly and will change His mind when they disappoint Him. But salvation does not rest on your performance. It rests on God's promise.

***"He who began a good work in you
will bring it to completion."***
— Philippians 1:6

If God started your salvation, God will finish it.
If grace began the story, grace will complete the story.
You are held by God's faithfulness, not your consistency.

This is why the gospel is good news: God does not quit what He starts.

CHAPTER 6: THE INVITATION — TURNING FROM SHADOWS TO LIGHT

Through this book we have walked through the collapse of "my truth." We've looked at the God who is holy, loving, and personal. We've been honest about the brokenness inside us. We've watched Jesus step into history to rescue sinners.

But information alone does not save.

You can learn about a parachute. You can admire the fabric. But if you're falling, none of it matters unless you pull the cord.

This chapter is not about learning more. It is about pulling the cord.

---

1. The Barrier — Why We Hesitate

If the gospel is such good news, why is it so hard to say "yes"? Most of the time, the barrier is fear.

We fear losing our autonomy. We fear losing our "authentic self." We fear being labeled "religious." But this fear is a lie.

C. S. Lewis—who fought God fiercely before surrendering—wrote:

"The more we let God take us over, the more truly ourselves we become—because He made us."

Surrender is not the death of who you are. It is the death of the mask you're tired of wearing.

---

2. The Great Resignation

To become a Christian is to resign from the job of being God.

For years, you've tried to save yourself. You've carried the weight of manufacturing your identity. You've tried to manifest peace, heal your own wounds, and prove your worth.

Are you tired yet?.

Repentance is simply handing in your resignation. It is saying: *"I am not the Captain. I am not the King. I am not the Center. And I don't want to be anymore."*.

This is not defeat. It is relief. Jesus said:

"Come to Me, all who labor and are heavy laden, and I will give you rest." — Matthew 11:28

The rest you long for begins when you stop trying to run the universe.

---

3. How to Receive Christ

There is no magic incantation. God is not impressed by poetic language. He listens to the posture of the heart.

Scripture gives the pattern plainly:

"If you confess with your mouth that Jesus is Lord and believe in your heart that God raised Him from the dead, you will be saved." — Romans 10:9

Receiving Christ involves two movements:

1. **Turning Away (Repentance):** Admitting you have been chasing false saviors—including the god of Self.

2. **Turning Toward (Faith):** Trusting that Jesus is who He says He is and did what He said He did.

You don't need to be in a church building. You don't need to be cleaned up first. You don't need to wait for a sign or a feeling.

If you are ready to stop running and start resting, you can do that right now.

---

4. A Prayer for the Exhausted Self-Creator

If you are ready to trust Christ, you can pray words like these. They are not magic. They simply express repentance and faith.

God, I am tired of being my own god. I admit I have lived by my own truth, and it has left me empty.

I confess I have sought peace in vibes, energy, and self-approval while ignoring You. I am sinful. My heart is broken, and I cannot fix it.

But I believe Jesus is Your Son. I believe He lived the perfect life I could not live. I believe He died for my rebellion. I believe He rose to give me new life.

Today, I stop running. I resign as the ruler of my life. Jesus, I receive You as my Savior and Lord. Forgive me. Cleanse me. Make me new. I am Yours.

---

5. What Just Happened?

If you prayed with honest faith, something massive just took place. Not a vibe. A verdict.

In the courtroom of heaven, the gavel came down: **Not guilty**.

- You are no longer spiritually dead—you are alive.

- You are no longer an orphan—you are a child of God.

- You are no longer defined by your past—you are a new creation.

You may feel a rush of emotion. Or you may feel nothing at all. Both responses are normal. A marriage is valid whether the bride cries or stands calmly. The validity comes from the covenant, not the emotion.

Your salvation rests on God's promise, not your feelings.

Jesus said:

"Whoever comes to Me I will never cast out." — John 6:37

He has you. And He will not let go.

---

6. You Are Not Alone — The Spirit Inside You

Here is the wildest part of the gospel: You are not merely forgiven—you are indwelt.

In every other religion, people reach up to God. In Christianity, God reaches down—and then moves in. The moment you trusted Christ, the Holy Spirit took up residence inside you.

He is not a feeling. He is not a mood. He is God Himself.

He brings two massive gifts:

- **He Stays:** In a world where people ghost you, the Spirit seals you permanently. He is not a visitor. He is a resident.

- **He Speaks:** Not with random impressions or vibes that contradict Scripture. The Spirit speaks through the written Word. He takes the black-and-white text of Scripture and turns it into technicolor reality in your heart.

Jesus promised:

"He will give you another Helper, to be with you forever… the Spirit of truth." — John 14:16–17

You never walk into a room alone again.

---

7. Moving Forward — How to Stay in the Light

Following Jesus is not about rule-keeping. It is about staying connected to the Person who rescued you.

Think of these practices not as laws, but as **lifelines**.

Listen (Scripture): God is not silent. He wrote a Book. Start with the Gospel of John. Read slowly. Read expectantly.

Speak (Prayer): Prayer is not a performance. You're talking to your Father. Tell Him your doubts, fears, and failures. He is not irritated by your voice. He welcomes it.

Belong (Church): You cannot follow Jesus alone. Find a church that opens the Bible and actually believes it. Don't search for a perfect church. Search for a faithful one.

---

8. A Final Word — The Hope That Holds You

If you take one truth from this chapter, make it this: Your hope is not in your grip on God. Your hope is in God's grip on you.

You will still have hard days. You will still fail. You will still wrestle with temptation and confusion. But you are no longer drifting. You are anchored.

The God who created galaxies now lives inside you. The Jesus who conquered death is writing your future.

You no longer have to be the hero of your story. The Hero has come. He has saved you. He is keeping you. And He will bring you all the way home.

Go live loved. Go live free. Walk in the Light.

CONCLUSION — THE DOOR IS OPEN

In this book you have heard the core of the gospel:

**You were made for God.
Sin broke what you could not fix.
Jesus came to do what you could never do.
Grace moved toward you.
Faith receives what grace gives.**

This entire book has been leading to a simple, honest moment:

What will you do with Jesus?

Not the aesthetic Jesus. Not the cultural Jesus. Not the distant Jesus.

The real Jesus—the One who lived, died, and rose again for you.

The Truth of the Gospel

But here is the truth the gospel shouts into every fragile heart:

Jesus never asked people to clean themselves up first. He simply said, **"Come to Me."**

"Come to me, all who labor and are heavy laden, and I will give you rest."
— Matthew 11:28

This Is Not About Religion—It's About Rescue

This is not about joining a religion.
This is not about promising perfection.
This is not about manufacturing spiritual feelings.

This is about acknowledging that God is sovereign.
And admitting He is God and you are not.
And recognizing that He works all things together for good.
And trusting Him.
And aligning your will to His.
And receiving what Christ has already done.

It is about saying yes to the One who has been pursuing you your entire life.

When you prayed and asked Jesus to be Lord of your life.

You were forgiven.
You were adopted.
You were made new.
You belong to Him now.

Not because you prayed perfectly. But because **Christ saves perfectly.**

"For everyone who calls on the name of the Lord will be saved."
— **Romans 10:13**

This Is Not the End—It's the Beginning

Salvation is not the finish line. It's the **starting line.**

The moment you trust Christ, everything changes—not because you become perfect, but because you become His.

And now the journey begins.

A journey of:

- **Learning** who God is through His Word

- **Growing** in grace through the Spirit's work
- **Fighting** sin with weapons you didn't have before
- **Belonging** to a family that spans eternity
- **Living** for a kingdom that will never end

This journey won't be easy. You'll stumble. You'll struggle. You'll doubt. You'll fail.

But you will not walk it alone.

"I am with you always, to the end of the age."
— **Matthew 28:20**

Jesus called the Holy Spirit "the helper", given to you when you accepted Christ as Lord. The Holy Spirit is fully God, the third person of the Triune God. He is with you, always.

Jesus doesn't save you and then abandon you. He walks with you. He leads you. He holds you. He carries you.

All the way home.

What Happens Next?

If you've just trusted Christ, here's what to do:

1. Tell Someone

Don't keep this to yourself. Tell a Christian friend, a pastor, a family member. Confession is part of faith.

"If you confess with your mouth that Jesus is Lord and believe in your heart that God raised him from the dead, you will be saved."
— **Romans 10:9**

2. Read the Bible

Begin with the Gospel of John. Let God's Word shape your new life.

"Your word is a lamp to my feet and a light to my path."
— **Psalm 119:105**

The Bible is God's revelation to humankind.

3. Find a Church

You need a local body of believers to walk with you. Don't try to do this alone.

"And let us consider how to stir up one another to love and good works, not neglecting to meet together..."
— **Hebrews 10:24-25**

A note of wisdom: Look for a church that holds to the authority of Scripture, the divinity of Christ, salvation by grace through faith, and the centrality of God's Word in worship. **A healthy church will point you to Jesus, not to subjective experiences or emotional manipulation.** In other words, **find a Bible-believing church where Christ is exalted and the Word is taught faithfully**.

4. Pray Daily

Talk to God. He's your Father now. He loves hearing from you.

"Rejoice always, pray without ceasing, give thanks in all circumstances..."
— **1 Thessalonians 5:16-18**

5. Consider Baptism

Baptism is a public declaration that you belong to Christ. It's symbolic of what Christ has done for you, raising you from death, cleansing you, and bringing you into a new life as a child of God.

"Go therefore and make disciples of all nations, baptizing them in the name of the Father and of the Son and of the Holy Spirit..."
— **Matthew 28:19**

If You're Still Uncertain

Maybe you've read this entire book, and you're still wrestling.

That's okay.

God is patient. He's not intimidated by your questions.

Keep seeking. Keep reading. Keep praying. Keep asking.

"You will seek me and find me, when you seek me with all your heart."
— **Jeremiah 29:13**

But don't mistake intellectual curiosity for neutral ground. There is no neutral ground with Jesus.

He is either Lord, or He is nothing.

C.S. Lewis said it best:

"A man who was merely a man and said the sort of things Jesus said would not be a great moral teacher. He would either be a lunatic—on the level with the man who says he is a poached egg—or else he would be the Devil of Hell. You must make your choice. Either this man was, and is, the Son of God, or else a madman or something worse."

You cannot reduce Jesus to a good teacher or a moral example. He claimed too much.

So the question remains: **What will you do with Him?**

A Prayer for the Journey Ahead

If you've trusted Christ and want to commit your journey to God, pray something like this:

"**Father, thank You for saving me.**
Thank You for adopting me, forgiving me, and giving me new life.
Help me grow. Give me a hunger for Your Word.
Surround me with people who love You.
Protect me from temptation. Strengthen me when I'm weak.
Teach me to walk in Your ways.
I am Yours. Lead me in the Light.
In Jesus' name, Amen."

The Truth That Holds

We began this book with a question:

Why does a world with endless choices leave us anxious instead of alive?

Now you know the answer.

Because **freedom without truth is chaos.**
Because **identity without foundation is exhausting.**
Because **meaning without God is illusion.**

We were made for something solid.

Not shifting preferences. Not subjective opinions. Not self-created meaning.

We were made for Truth—unchanging, unwavering, eternal.

And that Truth has a name: **Jesus Christ.**

"Jesus Christ is the same yesterday and today and forever."
— **Hebrews 13:8**

He is the foundation that will not crack.
He is the love that will not leave.
He is the truth that will not shift.
He is the grace that will not fail.

He is <u>Unwavering Love</u>.

And He is offering Himself to you—right now, right here, exactly as you are.

A Final Word

You were made for more than "my truth."

You were made for **the <u>Truth That Holds</u>.**

A truth that doesn't shift when you do.
A love that doesn't leave when you fail.
A foundation that won't crack when everything shakes.

That truth is Jesus.

And if you've trusted Him, you now stand on the most solid ground in the universe.

Not your feelings. Not your performance. Not your worthiness.

Christ's finished work.

You belong to Him now. And nothing—not sin, not Satan, not death itself—can snatch you out of His hand.

"For I am sure that neither death nor life, nor angels nor rulers, nor things present nor things to come, nor powers, nor height nor depth, nor anything else in all creation, will be able to separate us

from the love of God in Christ Jesus our Lord."
— **Romans 8:38-39**

This is the **unwavering** love you've been searching for your entire life.

And now you have it.

Not because of who you are.
But because of who He is.

Welcome home, beloved.

You are His.

Forever.

"He who began a good work in you will bring it to completion at the day of Jesus Christ."
— **Philippians 1:6**

Walk forward in confidence.

Not in yourself.

In Him.

Because grace doesn't just start the journey.

Grace finishes it. It means God will never leave you or forsake you. You can trust Him.

FURTHER READING

- **Piper, John.** *Fifty Reasons Why Jesus Came to Die*

- **Keller, Timothy.** *The Reason for God: Belief in an Age of Skepticism*

- **Platt, David.** *Radical: Taking Back Your Faith from the American Dream*

- **DeYoung, Kevin.** *The Hole in Our Holiness*

- **Sproul, R.C.** *The Holiness of God*

- **Ferguson, Sinclair B.** *The Whole Christ*

- **Dever, Mark.** *Nine Marks of a Healthy Church*

- **Grudem, Wayne.** *Christian Beliefs: Twenty Basics Every Christian Should Know*

THINK DEEP! SERIES

This series explores contemporary topics in culture, faith, and Christian living.

Made in the USA
Coppell, TX
18 February 2026

72033388R00036